God. How would you assess your relationship to God at this time? In what ways do you feel intimacy? distance? confusion? Note what has strengthened or weakened your bond this year.

#

Your parish. How would you rate your relationship with your community of believers? Do you worship, socialize, serve with them? Make some notes about your satisfactions and challenges.

#

Mission. You belong to a global community. How would you rate your concern for the earth and all its peoples? How have you contributed to your neighborhood? Do you communicate with civic leaders? Are you registered to vote? How have your faith and your actions made the world a better place this year?

#

Your work. Whether you are employed, homemaking, studying, retired, or unemployed, how would you rate your satisfaction with your work? Write some comments.

#	

Your finances. How do you rate your financial stability? In the past year, what causes have you had for thanksgiving or anxiety? Have you given to the needy and to those working for justice? Do you have a current will?

#	

Your education. Whether or not you are in school, you continue to learn by experience and development. How would you rate your educational progress this past year? Did it include religious education? What have you read? What stands out?

#	

The environment. Are you conscious of the ways you, your household and your community contribute to the care or the abuse of the earth's resources? What have you learned lately about these issues? What resource-conserving habits does your household practice—recycling, carpooling, turning off unneeded lights?

#

Your overall happiness. How would you rate your overall happiness? What are its principal sources and threats?

#

A blank box. Is there something else going on right now that these categories did not include? What is it? How would you rate your satisfaction with it? What notes do you want to make?

#

When you complete your assessments, read back over them and make sure they reflect who you are. Do they include the significant events, emotions, desires and accomplishments of the past year? Do they affirm you? Do they challenge you as well?

Before leaving your quiet space, thank God for your life. Ask God's forgiveness for your shortcomings. Thank God for the Spirit who has sustained you this past year and aided your meditation this day. Seek peace.

RENEWAL

Your next step is to make some plans for renewal this Lent. The decisions you make will build on your reawakened knowledge of yourself. They will help you shape a Lent that will fit your needs.

You may continue with this exercise immediately after you finish the previous one, but it might be better to take a break between these sessions so that you can enter into the next phase with a fresh spirit.

You will need a Bible.

Choose a quiet place and allow yourself plenty of time to complete the exercise. Calm your spirit, ask for God's help and begin.

First, open your Bible to the gospel passage, Matthew 6:1–18, and read the words. We hear this text every year on Ash Wednesday. Drawn from the Sermon on the Mount, it presents Jesus' practical advice about the spiritual life. He expects his followers to engage in three spiritual practices. These are prayer, fasting and works of charity and justice (often called almsgiving). Jesus wants us to be sincere in all three.

Then, as you plan your lenten renewal, concentrate on all three practices. They support one another. Praying will strengthen you for fasting and deepen your charity. Fasting will soften your heart for charity and quiet your spirit for prayer. Performing works of charity will give your fasting purpose and concentrate your prayer.

Review your assessments just before you start the next step. Then, as you go through the following sections, write down some ideas for prayer, fasting and almsgiving in the spaces provided. What you write will suggest some activities for this Lent.

Prayer

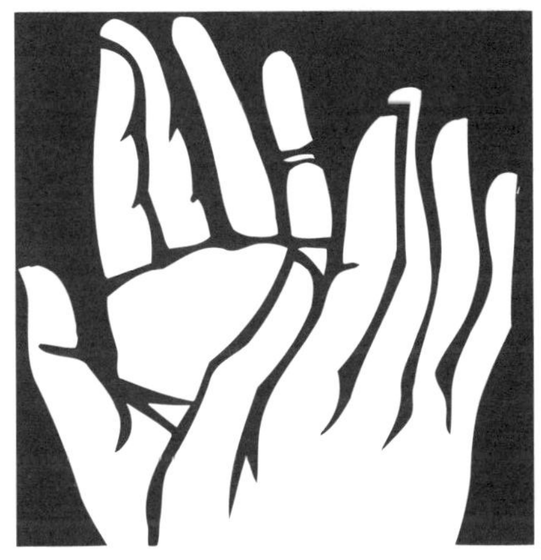

Sunday eucharist. The celebration of the Sunday eucharist is the heart of the entire spiritual life. It supports everything else. If your commitment to participating in the Sunday eucharist is at all weak, a resolution to strengthen it belongs at the top of your list.

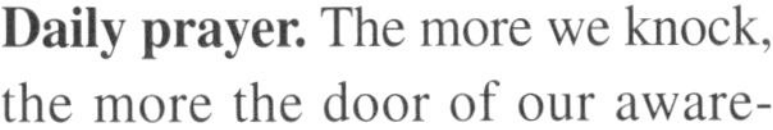

Daily prayer. The more we knock, the more the door of our awareness opens. How will you commit to daily prayer? What times of the day will work best for you? Mornings? Evenings? Do you have a special place for prayer? Some people designate a room for the purpose and furnish it in a way that invites prayer, including a Bible, prayer books, a chair or bench, a candle and perhaps some sacred images, incense or plants. Does your household pray together? Mealtimes and special events, as well as mornings and evenings—all are occasions when you might try gathering for prayer. Is your family comfortable with different forms of prayer? Lent is a good time to cherish the old and learn something new: reading a scripture passage slowly and prayerfully, meditative singing or chanting, the rosary, litanies, praying spontaneously, or sitting together in deep, rich silence. What reasonable goal could you and your household set this Lent?

Preparing for Sunday Mass. Do you prepare yourself for the Sunday liturgy each week? Do you read the scriptures beforehand so you can listen to them more attentively? Do you arrive at church early and stay for the end? Do you meet with friends to talk about this week's scriptures or about last week's homily? Do you meditate during the week, perhaps before the blessed sacrament?

Reading. Saint Benedict saw reading as a prayerful activity and required each of his monks to read a book during Lent. Whether you try scripture, biographies of saintly people, church teaching or something else about the spiritual life, reading can deepen your prayer.

Pilgrimage. Could you make a pilgrimage to a holy place to ritualize your spiritual journey? Is there a religious shrine or place of pilgrimage nearby? Could you visit a place holy to you—your birthplace, a former neighborhood, a place of natural beauty, your cathedral, the cemetery where loved ones are buried or the church where you were baptized? Could you walk the Stations of the Cross as part of your Lent this year, to follow the footsteps of Jesus?

As you reflect on these opportunities for prayer, consider those that might help you face some of the challenges that came to light from your assessments. You cannot carry out every idea. Which ones would help you the most this year? How might you open your ears in a new way to hear the voice of God?

I could renew my commitment to prayer in the following ways:

Fasting

Fasting means consuming less—or sometimes nothing. Abstinence means avoiding a certain kind of thing—such as meat or television. Both practices are hallmarks of Lent and they may be applied to a wide variety of things. Fasting and abstinence discipline the body to rely less

on the things of this world. They create within us a clear-headed dependence on God, whose love fulfills our every need.

Sometimes we fast from what is essentially good. We do so in a spirit of penance or to demonstrate our preference for the higher good of an unencumbered relationship with God. Other times we abstain from habits that hinder us—excesses we know we should trim, but struggle to do so. Both practices remove the distractions that keep us from the presence of God. During Lent we observe fast and abstinence to deepen our prayer and to open our hearts for charity.

Food. Fasting from food affects the body and shapes the human spirit. Here are the minimum expectations for most adult Catholics: On Ash Wednesday we are to fast by eating only one full meal and nothing between meals. On Ash Wednesday and all the Fridays of Lent we are to abstain from meat. These practices bind Catholics in a common but very small effort. (After Lent ends, we observe the paschal fast on Good Friday and Holy Saturday to prepare ourselves for Easter.)

If you are able, you may fast and abstain beyond that minimum. Jesus and Moses and Elijah fasted for forty days. Make some good decisions about what you will eat and drink, and when you will eat and drink for the next forty days.

What to eat and drink. Think of how to take good care of your body, a temple of the Holy Spirit. What do you eat and drink that you should abstain from? What has your doctor told you to eat more of and what less of? Is it time to lock the liquor cabinet, clip shut the bags of chips, tape closed the chocolates, purge the freezer of frozen treats? What choices can you make in solidarity with the poor? Eat less meat, less fish, less seafood. Choose grains and vegetables in place of animal foods to make the world more just. Prepare simple foods yourself. Learn to love these gifts of the earth and work of human hands. Make a delicious meatless soup every week, or a wonderful vegetable salad. Take time to marvel at earth's goodness.

When to eat and drink. Can you save your appetite for the times when the household can sit down together? Can you omit a meal or two each week? A little hunger will place you in solidarity with the poor of this world.

Fasting and abstaining will put you in touch with your body and its cravings, help you identify with the poor and hungry, strengthen your resolve, clear your thinking and make you more attentive to prayer and more thoughtful of others. If you share resolutions with your friends, you will discover the power of community in observing a lenten fast.

Exercise. Condition your body as you condition your soul. Including exercise as part of your lenten regimen will enhance the effects of your lenten diet. You'll find that you have more energy for prayer and service to others. Work out a plan with your friends and you'll have extra reasons to be faithful to your commitment.

Distractions and entertainments. If you give time this Lent to reading, to prayer and to good works, where will the time come from? Do you need to fast from time spent in front of screens? Television screens especially, but also computer screens. Television and the Internet can make genuine contributions to life, but they often serve our craving for distraction. Try setting them aside for a while and fill your life with more natural delights.

Other behaviors. Is this the time to fast from nicotine, alcohol, gambling, pornography? Are you behaving in some ways that do not conform to the moral standards of your faith? Are you unconsciously wasting resources? Are you neglecting something or someone in the crush of busyness? Besides food, how else should you fast and abstain this Lent to meet the challenge of your assessments?

I could renew myself through fasting in the following ways:

Almsgiving

God has given you all that you have—your life, your love, your abilities and resources. Count your blessings. Name the gifts you have received from your Maker.

The gifts God has given me include these:

Now recall the story of the widow's mite. Jesus, sitting by the Temple treasury one day, observed the people, rich and poor, making their offerings. A poor widow put in a small amount, yet Jesus singled her out as the example for his followers. She gave all she had.

Imagine Jesus as the usher in your church. Imagine Jesus combing the list of volunteers at your parish. Is he singling you out as an example for others? Do you give a little because it will help the needy for a while? Or do you give a lot because what God has given must be shared?

Time. We generally think of almsgiving as a financial contribution. But we can give our time and talent as well as our treasure. How might you give your time this season as a sign of your charity? Can you visit the sick or imprisoned? Can you pick up trash on your street, at your church or in public areas? Could you meet someone new at church each week? Could you send a complimentary letter to a friend? Are you someone's godparent? How might you spend quality spiritual time with your godchildren this season? Have you met the catechumens and elect of your community? Are you participating in parish social events? Do you attend neighborhood meetings? Do you contact those in public office to make your conscience heard on behalf of the needy in your area and around the world? What can you do with your time that will give alms this Lent?

Talent. With what skills has God endowed you? Do you put them at the service of others, not for pay but as gift? Are your talents at work in your home, your neighborhood, your civic community? Are they making a difference for the world? How could you use your talents this Lent?

Treasure. How do you share your treasure? The Bible recommends tithing, a contribution of ten percent to charity. What would ten percent of your gross income be? How close are you? Could you live on less if it meant you could feed a hungry neighbor? Who benefits from your generosity? Are you keeping up with your pledge to your parish? Are you a generous or a miserly tipper? What other donations could you make to charity? Can you forgive someone's debt to you? You are merely a steward of the treasure God has entrusted to you.

As you reflect upon these opportunities for almsgiving, which of them will help you as a Christian and support your other practices this Lent?

Time	Talent	Treasure

LENTEN RESOLUTIONS AND STRATEGIES

By now you should have quite a few ideas about how you might spend this Lent. It is time now to decide which you wish to accept for the season of renewal this year—what you want to add and what you want to subtract. Remember, you only have six weeks. Choose resolutions that you can accomplish and sustain. But make them challenging.

Follow your resolutions the entire six weeks. Or work into them gradually: Start with a modified version of your ideal the first week and reach your goal in the weeks ahead. Sharing your decisions with a trusted friend or advisor gives you a witness and supporter.

Even in the midst of Lent, Sundays are still celebrations of the Lord's day of resurrection. For this reason many people relax their lenten observances on Sundays. Others prefer to maintain their discipline throughout the six weeks so the entire season stands as a whole. It is your choice.

Some people choose activities simply because they are hard. Such choices will help build discipline, and if that is a personal goal it certainly has merit. But your lenten journey can also enhance other aspects of life. You can shape it to fit your spiritual needs and desires. Review your assessments. What resolutions will address the insights you have gained? Let Lent challenge you and fill you with delight.

The disciplines of Lent form individuals—but also the community. As you make your resolutions, Christians throughout the world will join you. Their pledges will lighten your journey.

When you re-evaluate yourself next year, you will see how, with God's help, you have made the world a better place. You will have kept Lent.

Now, mindful of the person you are, and of the person you would like to be, trusting that you are the child of a God who loves you as you are and empowers you to be more, write the resolutions you will make for Lent this year.

This Lent I Resolve:

To pray:

____

____

____

____

____

____

____

____

____

____

To fast:

To give alms:

COMMITMENTS TO KEEP

Use the day-by-day calendar of Lent on the next two pages to schedule the activities that will help you fulfill your plan. For example, you might write down your daily prayer times, the Bible study meetings you plan to attend at church, or the Saturday afternoons you've promised to volunteer at the soup kitchen. The calendar will help you remember what you intend to do and it will also serve as a log of your practices.

LENT

First Sunday		
Second Sunday		
Third Sunday		
Fourth Sunday		
Fifth Sunday		
Palm Sunday of the Lord's Passion		

h Wednesday **ENT BEGINS**			
	Holy Thursday **LENT ENDS** **TRIDUUM BEGINS**	Good Friday	Holy Saturday

SCRIPTURE JOURNAL

You began planning your renewal with the gospel reading from Ash Wednesday—Jesus' advice on prayer, fasting and almsgiving. Now you can use the readings for the Sundays of Lent as nourishment for your journey.

The gospels we hear at Mass on Sundays are organized in a three-year cycle. For convenience, we call them Year A, Year B and Year C. All the gospel readings for each Sunday of Lent are listed below.

When people preparing for baptism, the elect, are present in the assembly on the third, fourth and fifth lenten Sundays in any year of the cycle, the church reads the Year A gospels. These readings provide especially rich food for conversion. During those weeks, you may accompany the elect by meditating on these stories.

Read one gospel each week, then write about your journey through Lent.

FIRST SUNDAY OF LENT

Year A: Matthew 4:1–11
Year B: Mark 1:12–15
Year C: Luke 4:1–13

SECOND SUNDAY OF LENT

Year A: Matthew 17:1–9
Year B: Mark 9:2–10
Year C: Luke 9:28–36

THIRD SUNDAY OF LENT

Year A: John 4:5–42
Year B: John 2:13–25
Year C: Luke 13:1–9

FOURTH SUNDAY OF LENT

Year A: John 9:1–41
Year B: John 3:14–21
Year C: Luke 15:1–32

FIFTH SUNDAY OF LENT

Year A: John 11:1–45
Year B: John 12:20–33
Year C: John 8:1–11

PALM SUNDAY OF THE LORD'S PASSION

Year A: Matthew 27:11-54
Year B: Mark 15:1-39
Year C: Luke 23:1-49

THE SACRAMENT OF RECONCILIATION

Lent is always a good time to celebrate the sacrament of reconciliation, the church's proclamation of God's forgiveness of our sins.

"Sin is an offense against reason, truth, and right conscience; it is failure in genuine love for God and neighbor caused by a perverse attachment to certain goods" (*Catechism of the Catholic Church,* #1849). Sin wounds human nature and injures human solidarity.

To evaluate whether an action or desire is sinful, consider its object, intent and circumstances. What did you do? Why did you do it? How did you do it? If the action was wrong, if you did it on purpose and if no other factors intervened, admit your sin.

Every sin, no matter how private, affects others. Confessing your sin to a priest clarifies the social dimension of sin and allows you to receive pardon and peace through the ministry of the church. Your parish may offer the sacrament of reconciliation in a communal service sometime during the season. This underscores our bond with the community: We all struggle with sin and we are all blessed with God's mercy.

Or you may choose to meet privately with a confessor—either during a regularly scheduled time at your church, or during an appointment you arrange. Although you may choose any priest to hear your sins, and although you have the option of confessing anonymously, consider celebrating the sacrament this time face to face, to a priest you know, a shepherd of souls who cares for you. If you make an appointment, your priest may have more time to hear your reflections, offer you counsel and rejoice with you at the marvels God is doing in your life.

In anticipation of this Lent, you reflected on your strengths and weaknesses as a person. You brought to mind the parts of your life you would like to put behind you, and the parts you wish you could develop. By bringing these reflections to the sacrament of reconciliation, you allow the saving love of Jesus Christ to flood your heart, the strengthening grace of the Holy Spirit to support you in your weakness and the generous embrace of your Creator to restore you once again.

The point of the disciplines of Lent is conversion of heart, conversion to the gospel. Seal that conversion with a celebration of reconciliation, and experience the peace that comes from hearing the words of absolution.

Find out when the sacrament is offered at your parish this year. Make its celebration a cornerstone of your lenten renewal.